Grandma's Haiku Passages for Youth

Written by Connie Holt
Cover by retired artist Sharon Revell

No part of this publication may be reproduced, stored in a retrieval system, or transmitted in any form or by any means, electronic, mechanical, photocopying, recording or otherwise, without permission of the author or publisher.

For information regarding permission, write to Starla Enterprises, Inc.
Attention: Permissions Department,
740 W. 2nd, Ste. 200, Wichita, KS 67203

First Edition

ISBN: 978-0880-6609-6

Text copyright @ 2022 by Connie Holt
Cover copyright @ 2022 by Sharon Revell

All rights reserved.
Published by Starla Enterprises, Inc.

Printed in the U.S.A.

HOPE

If you have no dreams

Your future may look too dim-

Dream a million dreams.

Believe me on this-

Ten years from now, bullies failed;

The world's your oyster!

Your required reading-

The "Little Engine That Could,"

Don't ever give up!

When you interview,

Shoulders back, smile, be truthful.

The job can be yours!

Times are sometimes hard.

Please don't lose your faith and hope-

Morning brings the sun.

Seek out your future,

You have a purpose in life.

Go find your passion.

You have the choice to;

Complain, quacking like a duck,

Or soar like eagles!

March to your own beat.

You have time to discover,

Who you truly are.

Travel when you can.

It opens your soul and mind

To the Whole Wide World!

Be like a squirrel,

Save up for the leaner times.

Save yourself worry.

Sorrow may find you,

Perhaps when you least expect,

But Joy will return.

If you have children,

Celebrate their day of birth,

And hug them daily.

Feeling somewhat down?

Give a hug and get a hug-

Instant mood lifter!

A true friend is worth

Much more than silver or gold,

Be true in return.

I hope your lifetime

Brings you joy and happiness,

People who love you.

LIFE

Sticks and stones may scar,

But their words cannot slay you-

You know who you are!

Stay anchored to Truth.

Let your name be known to all

As a Straight Arrow.

Embarrass yourself?

It happens to everyone

Let it go and laugh.

You say you are bored?

Let a book take you away,

Your mind is the jet!

Always know your name

Is your most prized possession.

Stay honorable.

All good intentions

Sail off as leaves in the wind,

If not acted upon.

Did you say you are bored?

Unleash imagination-

Become a writer.

What is your talent?

Try your hand at many things.

Find one that fits.

Buy really good shoes.

After all, your feet take you

To all of your dreams!

Ask a grandmother

How to sew on a button,

It can save your clothes.

Check out sales at stores.

It's fun and satisfying-

Never pay full price.

Keep these magic words

"Please and thank you, I'm sorry,"

On tip of your tongue.

Run barefoot through grass,

Grounding yourself to the earth,

Feeling like a child.

It is a cliché,

But education is key

To follow your dreams.

You're called a Pansy-

Say, "Thank you," for they survive,

The tough winter storms.

The wise seek knowledge,

The fools hunger for gossip.

Always choose wisely.

Be a safe driver

By taking Drivers Ed class-

Never text and drive!

Reading can take you

From deep, dark seas to the heights-

Travel of the mind!

As much as you can,

Try hard to be kind and fair.

Yet sometimes you'll fail.

Avoid evil ones,

They take you down crooked paths

That may never end.

Nature's alarm clock

Awakens you at seven-

Bird a capella!

LOVE

Time is on your side,

When it comes to being loved.

True love takes some time.

It's so very true;

To have a friend, be a friend-

Always uplift them.

When you least expect,

Someone will ask you to dance-

Perhaps forever!

Forgive your Loved ones.

Tomorrow is not promised.

Don't burden your heart.

Are you spurned in Love?

You can't make someone love you.

'Twas not meant to be.

Give parents a break!

After all, they lacked training,

Starting on Day One!

Your grandma asks you,

"Please do not text while driving"-

Show your love, obey!

Find a job you love,

And work can be so much fun,

You won't grow weary.

Cardinals thrill me!

I often spy them feeding.

God favors Sparrows!

Whisperer of birds

And sundry woods animals;

Listen in silence.

Forgiveness is good.

Without it, your stomach churns,

So let grudges go.

Narcissist stares,

Looking in your trustful eyes,

But does not see You!

Spend time alone,

Listening to the birds sing

And watch the flowers preen.

This is the second Haiku collection published by Connie Holt.

Grandma's Haiku For Children is still available.